THE
OTHER SIDE
OF THE OFFICE

**Dedicated to my two adorable
Sons' Will and Robbie**

Order this book online at www.trafford.com
or email orders@trafford.com

Most Trafford titles are also available at major online book retailers.

Note for Librarians: A cataloguing record for this book is available from Library
and Archives Canada at www.collectionscanada.ca/amicus/index-e.html

Printed in Victoria, BC, Canada.

ISBN: 978-1-4251-9010-1 (Soft)
ISBN: 978-1-4251-9012-5 (e-book)

*We at Trafford believe that it is the responsibility of us all, as both individuals
and corporations, to make choices that are environmentally and socially sound.
You, in turn, are supporting this responsible conduct each time you purchase a
Trafford book, or make use of our publishing services. To find out how you are
helping, please visit www.trafford.com/responsiblepublishing.html*

*Our mission is to efficiently provide the world's finest, most comprehensive
book publishing service, enabling every author to experience success.
To find out how to publish your book, your way, and have it available
worldwide, visit us online at www.trafford.com*

Trafford rev. 7/7/2009

 www.trafford.com

North America & international
toll-free: 1 888 232 4444 (USA & Canada)
phone: 250 383 6864 ♦ fax: 250 383 6804 ♦ email: info@trafford.com

THE OTHER SIDE OF THE OFFICE

Anyone who has ever worked for a recruitment agency as a temporary PA/Secretary should be able to relate to and empathise with my following observations and experiences over many years working as a temp. You certainly have to be a particular type – peculiar, or maybe just plain mad. You have to be able to change and adapt on a regular basis in any situation and environment you are thrown into. In fact, the word that springs to mind is chameleon!

You have to learn to quickly adapt to different places and sometimes strange personalities and, believe me, I've encountered both!

Besides being a qualified secretary, I am also a qualified teacher of movement, dance complementary therapy and offer relaxation and stress management courses. So having taught all these other skills has certainly helped me when I have come up against the *stress head* boss, premenstrual fellow secretary or indeed, the *menopausal*.

You have to offer an ear to everyone and effectively become the office counsellor, sit on the fence where office politics are rife, and put up with lots of different personalities and age groups. The bitchiness, the moods, and, of course, the listening skills are acquired as a result of, for example, listening to the occasional odd bod. The one who drones on about being fed up and disillusioned by their colleagues, but who is too frightened or lazy to make any life changes to get another job!

It's important from time to time to remember to GET OUT OF THAT BOX! Stretch, challenge yourself, MOVE ON!

Occasionally, you will come across an enlightened one, one whose personality is similar to your own. I recall how much fun it was to work in the seventies and eighties: people then didn't live to work, they worked to live. It's all too serious now, no one laughs anymore. How times have changed – and not, in my opinion, for the better.

Humour is a rare thing and no one has a good belly laugh in the workplace anymore. If you do engage in a bit of banter then you are considered as not being 'focused' on your work and being frivolous. Read Robert Holden and his laughter clinic. I worked with him years ago before he became famous.

I adopt my chameleon mode and genuinely try to fit into any environment. Although to be honest, my natural zany personality can often be a drawback; people take offence. Well it doesn't matter to me what they think. I really don't give a toss.

I always make it my business to get on with everyone. But let's face it, that's not always possible. When I'm involved in some particularly boring assignment I can quite easily act as though I'm brain dead or something, which definitely helps. That way, I can at least give the impression that I am enjoying myself, albeit in a dozy sort of way, and hope the agency gets me another assignment.

I'm definitely a stickler. I never fall at the first hurdle and often stick at an assignment way beyond the call of duty and to the detriment of my mental health. Let's face it, I'm an older lady of … erm… a certain number of years.

One day though, all of this will affect my sanity. There is always an inner glow and a feeling of confidence that reminds me I don't have to stay in one place. I have the balls to move on and then it will be *adios*, you sad buggers.

Despite all this negativity, there are places in which I would have loved to have remained such as the Police, Charities, and Social Services. Work that one out. But *never, ever* pompous solicitors' offices…yuk!

But I must not include Tim, a young solicitor from Thompsons', full of life and a really interesting person. Moreover, there was a common denominator that forged a friendship between us in the short time I worked there: by a strange coincidence we had both read – him for the first time and me for a second some years later – Sallinger's *Catcher in the Rye*. Good lad!

Golden Rules

- Never be yourself
- Appear more intelligent than you really are
- Have your own opinions (especially in solicitors' offices)
- Know too much about PCs
- In general, have more experience and qualifications than some of the morons you work for or with
- Tone yourself down, don't dress like a hippy, always dress formally
- Personality: if you have one, and they don't, then lose it
- Outrageous sense of humour: if you have one, and they don't, lose it

- Sort out the first day of your assignment: Which of the office staff are the lazy mares? And remember, don't let them palm off on to you all the additional, boring work
- Not to mention the mountains of filing that they can't be arsed to do
- Remember that for them the mention of getting a temp in means "whoopee, get your feet up time, we can have a rest!"
- Smile at all times through gritted teeth as you won't be staying
- Bear in mind that in some cases there are assignments where you would love to stay, it's not all doom and gloom

So that's about it, really. I learned the hard way but me being the type of person I am, I had a lot of fun along the way, as my memories of the following assignments will hopefully indicate. I can remember them as if they happened yesterday ...

The Journey to Work

As ever, my workday journey sets off from the train station and I just love the misty, grey, dark, dank wintry mornings when there is nothing nicer than being on the train; snuggled up daydreaming, staring out of the window, and wearing a blank, gormless, baggy-eyed, pale-faced expression.

I don't do mornings as it takes me an hour to wake up properly so the train is the perfect place to do this. I love to look out onto the misty grey, spring-like fields, staring at the large, circling, ugly black crows, with their huge shiny beaks, busily building their nests in the tall trees as the train chugs by them.

These sturdy nests sway precariously in the breeze as the predators in the sky circle around them. Khaki-coloured sheep are dotted about, nibbling what remains of the grass, looking cold and dirty. I gaze at the remnants of soggy autumn leaves, tumbling down deep embankments towards the train track.

As the train enters into a long dark tunnel, I become aware of something that never, ever ceases to startle me. I'm dreamily dozing out of the window and the darkness is acting as a mirror.

My scary-looking white face stares back and I am appalled to see how awful my make-up looks. But enough of that, my thoughts are now on my new assignment.

As I trundle on towards Leeds, I observe people's heads tucked into paperbacks, reading the *Metro News*, some zombified with their ipods playing, some dozing, some speaking loudly into their mobiles – which, incidentally, I find bloody annoying as I am still trying to catch up on my kip!

Some are yawning with their mouths so wide open you can see all their decayed teeth, fillings and even their clackers. Why don't people these days cover their mouths when they yawn? I was always taught to!

All these germs make me think I must get out my essential aromatherapy oils and dab on rosemary around my hair and shoulders so I don't get their airborne bacterial infections. Rosemary killed off the Black Plague you know! And yes, I am neurotic!

Wafts of different perfumes pervade the train and hammer the old olfactory system. I sit there trying to guess them all, which evokes memories of perfumes that were fashionable during my youth and of course 'Angel' perfume now seems to be the most popular choice. An apt name as I used to work for the Office Angels Recruitment Agency. Must buy some!

As the train approaches Leeds I glance down at the canal and see barges rocking gently. They look so tranquil and peaceful among the wet surroundings and I wonder if the occupants are still in the land of nod, with great big hangovers from the previous Sunday evening. Oh, how I would love a barge, but I don't know about the isolation. I no longer have my wonderful Al, my deceased Golden Labrador, to protect me – he was bloody useless anyway, more focused on food!

As we head further into the city, walls appear adorned with multi-coloured and creative graffiti. The graffiti isn't unpleasant, however; it consists of some pretty amazing artwork, rather than the usual tedious array of swear words. It makes me want to take it up myself, buy some psychedelic spray paint and have a bash.

The downside to travelling by train is that you are all packed in like sardines and therefore more likely to catch colds and flu, hence the rosemary.

Then there's the rank farts that often permeate the train, the ones that people try to slip out without them being noticed but I must admit that I too have been guilty of that a few times! Then there's the bad breath. When people yawn they release an air pollutant. Such environmental saboteurs should be banned from trains without exception.

The solitude – no-one seems to want to speak these days – is quite sad, but at the same time peaceful if you are a dozy head first thing in the morning. I can drift off into my own world, or just watch people and the world go by. And another big plus is that you can get through loads of paperbacks, which is a hell of a lot safer now I travel on the train as I used to read in the car while driving to work! Then there's the odd bod that occasionally tries to stare me out and sometimes wins, especially if they look a little pervie, which this peculiar, French-looking man does. More of Monsieur du Pont later.

Picking noses in full view is also a very common sight; the culprits try to hide behind

11

their books or irritating lap-tops which also, along with mobiles, should be banned from trains in the morning and returned only for use in the evenings. On second thoughts, perhaps not. I'm with Bob Geldof there! Getting anti-email, etc! The final tanoy announcement is made for my destination, Leeds, so I'm heading for my new assignment, Bart & Co. Hey ho, here I go!

Assignment One : Fart & Co

I arrive at the reception area of Bart & Co Solicitors. There to greet me are three middle-aged prim ladies.

All around me are ill-matched carpets and odd-looking seating. Yes, many solicitors are so cheap and cheerful unless they are a huge company. The flash of the receptionists' plastic dentures almost blinds me and what with their busy attire, I feel quite overwhelmed. This is an exceptionally busy office where the phones never seem to stop, but the most hysterical thing is how these ladies answer the phone. Although, granted, they are fairly well spoken, when they answer the phone they assume this awful posher-than-posh, high-pitched voice and announce "Bart and

Company, good morning", or "Bart and Company, good afternoon."

Such snobbery in the air, it almost feels as if they are accusing the client of ringing the company and bothering them, even though it is the inconsiderate clients who pay their wages!

Like many small practices, all the machinery is old, notably the ancient PCs. Everything is falling to bits; three legs on a desk, for example, with the missing 'leg', which is no more than a pile of old legal books.

I arrive at my desk on this, the first day of my many assignment, to find four or five huge

piles of client files on the floor with dictaphone tapes on each pile. There is no "give us yer coat" or "hello, how are you?" Nothing of the kind. I just sit down, the secretaries point at the work and I "got stuck in". I soon realise the staff here are particularly bone idle and are just so ignorant. There is no "there's the loo, there's the coffee." This has to be one of the grimmest places I have ever worked in.

But I must emphasise that not all companies are like this and it does get better. There was one particular secretary I observed and, let's face it, if a temp comes in and she's good (and I put myself in that category) the work certainly does accumulate and they tend to put their feet up. I started one morning at the usual time of 9am and this particular secretary was already there. She stood in the doorway until 9.50, while I rattled off all the work. Legal work can be very exhausting and demanding. It was reminiscent of a Taiwanese sweat shop.

Anyway, a couple of hilarious things happen on this actual day.

I go up to the ladies toilet and into one of the cubicles, close the door and to my amazement, on the back of the door, is a set of do's and don'ts of the disposal of sanitary wear written by the (female, of course) Senior Partner.

There are about 20 bullet points on what to do and what not to do with soiled sanitary wear and I just can't stop laughing at the thought of someone with nothing better to do than write such stuff!

The devil inside me arises as it often does, and I can't resist adding to the bottom of the list, *Someone obviously hasn't enough to do.* The following day I find myself hauled in front of the Senior Partner for doing such a thing. I try to explain it was just a joke but she obviously doesn't see the funny side of it as I am getting ticked off at my age. How dare they, the sad sods!

The week progresses, the work piles up even more and the other secretaries get lazier and lazier until one day the snobby receptionists ask me if I will kindly relieve them on reception for a couple of hours in the afternoon (as if I don't have enough to do).

One of them, they claim, is going to the dentist. Marvellous! So there I am, on my own, dreamily gazing out of the window, when the phone rings. I just can't resist it. I pick up the phone, take a deep breath and in their very own high-pitched, snobby voice I announce to the client, "Good afternoon, Fart and Company."

The client at the other end says, "I beg your pardon!"

"Bart and Company," I haughtily reply, in a 'how dare you question my salutation?' sort of way. Anyway, that really amuses me for the rest of the afternoon and I do it twice more for good measure. When the receptionists come back I revert to my good old, ultra-professional self.

I wasn't sorry to leave there; to summarise, crappy old machinery, old PCs, lazy secretaries and arrogant female partners with no sense of humour. Still, apart from that, it paid the mortgage and bills and kept the wolf from the door!

The Office Temp Poem

A little apprehension on my first day
No one to welcome, no one to say
There's the coffee and oh yes, there's the loo
Oh yeah, love, and there's you
As they point to my seat at the other side of the
office

The nameless office temp manages a smile
Smart and chirpy, to stay for a while,
Stacks of dreary work, ceiling high
And all that filing to come, oh, one big sigh!

The temp, of course, will do all the dross
'Cos they'll all get their feet up to have a rest
No office induction, no Hi, how are you?
She gets all the duff jobs that they won't do

The work is so boring and here comes more
A mind-numbing day, yes, one big bore
Sat here it's so wearisome, I want some fun
Think I'll go off and photocopy my bum

Office politics, blimey they do fall out
No-one to talk to, I might just shout
I could glance out of the window, watch the
clouds roll by

Then I'll be reported by those so lazy, so lazy...
so sly!

Again, no mention of coffee, tea or lunch
And where's the loo you miserable bunch?
Sat there typing, no-one swaps a word
This job's just rotten, it's quite absurd

Surely, temp, this will not do!
You have a split-infinitive in this line, you silly
moo."
You wot, mate, your 'aving a laugh
No, on second thoughts, they don't do that here,
do they!

And by the way, the name's Jan

A lazy secretary, getting her feet up!

Other strings to my bow

Monsieur du Pont, a very French-looking man, complete with (would you believe?) a black French beret and a dirty old mac, but without the obligatory onions around his neck, boards the train.

Once he is seated he has a terrible habit of staring at me! Is it my stunning beauty, I constantly ask myself, or my divine, shiny red lips, courtesy of Rimmel, which I painstakingly apply each morning before I face the world? He wears the beret on what appears to be a balding head. His clothes aren't particularly fresh and look old and worn in parts, daubed with, if you look closer whilst he's not looking, camembert cheese! NO CANNOT BE!

I feel uncomfortable as we have this staring out competition and I do believe, in quite a smug way, that I am probably the one female on the train who can stare him out the longest. I think it's down to my more senior years.

This particular morning, he has started to enjoy himself, and is now taking on the aura of a pervert. And it's now getting worrying for me because I am rising to the challenge. I must seek help.

Anyway, I purposely keep looking out of the window to observe the lovely wooded areas through which the train travels, but there is something inside me that cannot resist having a look at Monsieur and yes, he is still staring at me.

I can get my own back though and look at him at leisure when the train goes through a tunnel and the window then becomes the mirror again; that way I can stare at him to my heart's content.

How have I got my own back? Because I now know that he knows that I know that he knows... For God's sake, Jan, get a life – here comes the station and off I jolly well go to what's next. Oh yes, my other talents gained while I've been temping have proved invaluable!

I have never, ever, got my head around why people stay in dead end jobs all their lives. We have just one bite of the cherry and these days I think it's essential to be multi-talented, because if something does not work out in one area then you always have a backup and other paths. Besides being a trained PA and Secretary dogs body, and teacher in adult and further

education, which I have done for years, I added other strings to my bow many years ago by training in complementary therapies, first starting in Hong Kong whilst I lived there with my two young sons, Will and Robbie and solicitor husband (the first one, husband that is!).

I am fortunate that I have not given up secretarial work. For a few years I had a beautiful relaxation retreat in the North Yorkshire Moors and this was such an exciting and rewarding adventure to undertake. It took a lot of very hard

work and long hours, but it was such a delight to see people change their lives. Worn out people would travel far and wide to our delightful haven in the moors. I offered a full itinerary for the weekend where I taught movement (yes, I'm trained in that too), complementary therapies and relaxation classes. I was lucky to have trained with the Health Education Authority in the 80s and acquired these skills. At that time people were better looked after in Adult and Further Education and the same was true in the workplace.

Having studied in these areas for almost 28 years, I often take these skills into the workplace and any temps reading this please take note: if I ever got any 'stress heads', in other words stressed out bosses, I always used to incorporate my treatments either by burning oils, giving treatments (such as head massages and reflexology) or giving away free relaxation CDs teaching visualisation and neuro-muscular techniques.

I know I must appear rather strange to a lot of people when I am out there temping but I am always aware, much more so than in the 80s, that we live in a faster, busier, hi-tech-in our faces world. Mobiles, emails, PCs and the like; there is never any time for ourselves. I feel that people are far more aggressive and angry. I hope that whatever I produce in the workplace will assist in calming people down and make it a nicer, happier, more relaxed environment to work in.

Burn-out is so on the cards for most people and I believe our world is now a far too busier place. I am on a one-man mission to make people have a balanced work/life existence. Will I succeed I ask myself

I do think that some people find it difficult to accept my kind of mad, exuberant, wild and amusing personality, along with this person who is quite free to give treatments such as aromatherapy and reflexology during lunch breaks. And there's another story: people do not, or are scared to, take lunch breaks these days. This is such a false economy for our well being, we end up with crappy life styles – just no work/life balance whatsoever. I work to live, I certainly do NOT live to work!!

I am far more spiritual than religious, so if I can do someone a good deed then I will always try and incorporate something during my lunch time. I have even taught relaxation sessions in a half hour lunch break and the difference that it makes is incredible. Can you imagine if you did that a few times per week? What an amazing society we would have. My good old mate Gaynor Faye, actress and Buddhist, is so much into the work/life balance. If we get out of kilter, we meet up, relax, meditate and off we go again for our next challenges. But having a truly wonderful family and friends is so important to us both. Oh, did I mention the red wine helps too!

Assignment Two: Too Old to Dance

Now old Mustard Coat who gets on the same train as me is a very rotund lady, who I am sure is a very, very nice person, but rather scary. You get the distinct feeling that she does not want to sit next to anyone on this planet whilst journeying through to Leeds! Her mustard coat is in fact one of those puffer-type jackets so it makes her twice the size, takes up twice as much seat and not only invades my space but takes over my own part of my seat.

So there I am, sitting with my shoulders hunched and knocked-kneed while she reads her Metro Paper, her arms outstretched in my face. She is reading with such startling haste and speed, turning each page at a savage pace that at times feels very threatening and certainly disturbs my slumber. And when she has finally huffed and puffed her way through the paper she sits there in a crossed arm posture looking rather cross. If I was a bit braver I might strike up a conversation with her. I will one day. She is probably very nice. There's a loud announcement to tell me that I have arrived at the station and to my next assignment. So what's on the cards for me now? It involves some very hands-on people. Hurrah!

Probably the best place I've worked at is Social Services. An environment full of fabulous women and a couple of fabulous guys, mainly Steve and Gary. Great men, the two of them, one doing work for the blind and the other for the deaf. They are particularly welcome in my own case as I have tinnitus in my left ear and poor eye sight in my right eye. Steve tried to teach me how to use sign language without, I must confess, much success. But I was so fascinated when he conversed with any member of the public who came to the office who happened to be deaf or who had hearing difficulties. He was amazing to watch. There was also a very supportive group of women, most of them social workers and secretaries, headed by Maggie who supported us all in every way possible. In particular, they were responsible for drawing up the care plans for the elderly, some in hospital and others in their own homes.

One of the funniest and craziest secretaries was Christine Burn, whom I nicknamed Mother Earth. Chris was a very hands-on person and looked after us all in one way or another. She also had a sense of humour very similar to mine. When things got very hectic and fraught (as they did frequently) we would cope in our own zany way by employing large quantities of silliness. An example of this would be Chris's daily rendition of 'Happy Talk' which, if I remember correctly, comes from the timeless *South Pacific* movie. This was one of our most amazing stress busters. We would sing out loud whilst typing when the pressure was building. One of our favourites was by the Corrs 'This man is cracking up' but we would sing 'These girls are cracking up'.

One day Chris answered a phone call and instead of putting it on hold she left the receiver on the desk to go in search of Maggie and I was at my desk singing Hot Chocolate's 'I believe in miracles'. Who should be on the other end of the phone but one of the managers from one of the other areas who was less than chuffed with my melodic tones; so much so that she told Maggie. Fortunately, Maggie stuck up for me and said, "There are times when staff morale is pretty low to start with without making it any lower." Good old Maggie!

It was a very hands-on environment to work in and a lot of the phone calls were from the elderly, so you had to be sympathetic and empathise with the clients.

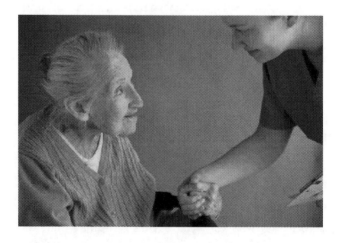

I had a brain wave one day and was quite tempted to act upon it but I probably would have got the sack and maybe even arrested. My plan was to escape for the day, hire a double decker bus and go around all the old people's homes that we looked after, kidnap (well old people nap) them and take them all on an outing to the coast. We could have worn funny hats, annoyed folk with those blowy-squeaky things, drunk crates of ale, and had a fabulous sing song. Off to Blackpool to dance! To see the tower! It is a most enjoyable and satisfying job working as a secretary for the Social Services; and hats off to the social workers and staff who work relentlessly day-in and day-out with the elderly and all their needs. I did have fun there and recognised the tensions so I took it upon myself to entertain the staff. I did introduce free acupressure treatments during our lunch breaks, partnership head massage and the odd relaxation class. A treat for everyone!

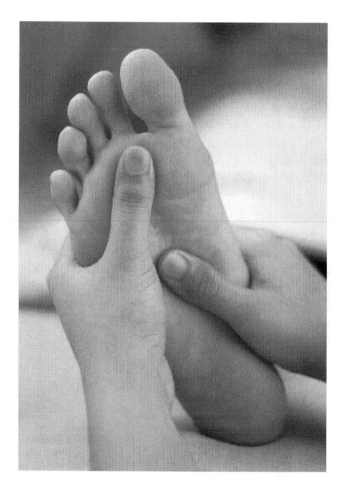

Happy Feet!

One day I got my usual call from a lovely Miss Black who was a resident at one of the homes. We would laugh, chat, have a bit of mutual leg-pulling, to lift her spirits and keep her cheerful. One day I threatened to take her to the Blackpool Tower as I had recently watched a TV programme on old fashioned ball room dancing. Miss Black responded with "Oo, I don't know about that, my dear, I think by now I'm too old to dance!" I could have asked her to go bungee jumping with me and she would have entered into the spirit of such an absurd suggestion by bursting into a hearty and thoroughly healthy laugh. However, it's one thing being elderly and physically frail but quite another to be mentally frail and unbeknown to me at the time, a scary but challenging assignment was looming on the horizon in the form of a psychiatric hospital.

A big lad aged around ... let me see ... 35 or so. A well-built lad who pushes and shoves his way onto the train each morning, sporting a David Beckham-type jewelled ear ring. He invariably wears the same dull and non-descriptive clothes and you can guarantee his mobile will be glued to his ear. He doesn't talk particularly quietly and it's nearly always his mum he's talking to, the conversation going something like this:

"No, No, Mam, don't do mi tea toneet 'cos I'm off out with some of the lads from work and I'll probably have a skin full." Pause. "Well I didn't know that you were going to Morrison's to do a big shop!" A much lengthier pause. Lots of hmms then he loses contact as we go through a tunnel. Happily, I drift off again trying to think whether I have left any incriminating evidence at my last assignment, such as all my personal correspondence on the shared drive, emails to my mate Gaynor and all the stuff I do when I'm bored witless. Big Lad's mobile sounds again.

"For God's sake, Mother, don't cook for me, I'll be reet! I'll get a kebab and poison missen. No, ar said no, and no, I don't want a bloody pudding." The train is now shaking with laughter! At this point the train enters big lad's stop and as usual he is first to dive off the train, quickly followed by me and half of the passengers, just in case he gets that third call from his mum. I lose him in the crowd but then realise I'll probably get him on the train coming home.

I chirp up with the realisation that this week's assignment is very near to the train station, so that's a plus; no long trek and just enough time to buy myself that much-needed caffeine lift from Burger King. Yes, just a coffee. I don't eat junk food, honestly, Mr Jamie Oliver. Thank God you changed school dinners.

Assignment 3 :   Terror at Mandalay

With its long, dark, sweeping and imposing
driveway, this psychiatric unit I worked at   in
Leeds, a place I will always remember with great
love and affection. I jest! I will always remember

this eerie foreboding Victorian establishment with great trepidation. Not quite perched on the top of a cliff, like Mandalay in Daphne de Maurier's 'Rebecca', but a similar foreboding place!

This Victorian institution no longer stands and has become a modern housing estate, a good thing too if you ask me. The place was dark, dingy and depressing and I was always surprised that anyone ever got better as a result of having stayed there. It was a three-month booking and I was looking forward to a longish assignment to get my teeth into, something interesting, and I did initially enjoy this post until I met the dreaded Millie who was one of the canteen staff – or so I thought. The staff canteen was huge and sprawling like the rest of the place and on this particular day as I went in for my lunch I noticed it was totally empty, not even any staff – obviously they were doing different shifts. I'll never forget being at that place. There are some things you just never forget, no matter how hard you try…

I sat down with a delicious subsidised lunch and start to acquaint myself with the surroundings. After a few minutes this largish rotund, pale-faced girl plonks herself next to me and, after introducing herself as Millie, starts to engage me in conversation. I thought it strange at the time that she should come and sit next to me, mainly because the place was completely empty, but just assumed that she was in need of a bit of company.

I soon begin to pick up vibes that I was not, in fact, chatting to one of the staff, but, ... to one of the inmates! And before I realised who she was, she has within minutes extracted lots of personal information from me, my name and which office and department I worked in.

The following day, with my office window wide open on this glorious summer's day, I hear the dulcet tones of Millie shouting my name. Much to my relief there were two other ladies who work in the same office and were obviously used to her behaviour. One of them goes to the window and shouts down to her to go back to her ward, muttering as she goes back to her desk, "She probably hasn't taken her medication."

Over the following couple of weeks, the uneasiness that Millie seems to have over me grows stronger and stronger. I see her hovering around the grounds waiting for me, I have to do a quick exit at lunch time or in the evenings so she can't see me. The one thing on my side is that she is overweight and can't shift like I can over the centre green! All that running paid off.

A few weeks go by and not having seen Millie for a time I assume she must have been sedated for a while. On this particular night, I'm clearing up my desk and closing down my PC. I think I hear a noise, but carry on. I'm on my own as the other two ladies have gone home for the evening. I decide it's probably best to take my escape route, which was the old servants staircase, the one the staff didn't use that often, unless they're going down to the rear car park, which was the car park that I used.

After making sure the doors and windows were locked and the lights out I descended the back staircase. Then, as I come to the last but one level, I get the shock of my life. Millie jumps out at me! Every horror movie, 'Psycho', 'Don't Look Now', and the film with the beautiful Audrey Hepburn in which she plays a blind woman and accidentally gets involved with some drug smugglers. All rolled into one! How the hell do I get out of this? Leg it, and be quick about it!

I feel the tremor in my voice as I demand that Millie return to her ward, but she becomes aggressive and angry towards me, saying that I had been deliberately avoiding her (come on, who wouldn't?). I back off slowly, pretending to retrace my steps, but swing around and shove her out of the way so I can make my escape. I am out of the car park door like a bullet and, thank God, into my clapped out 5-series BMW, central locking. My hands are shaking so much so that I can't get the key in the car lock. I look down into the car and see I've got to remove the crook lock, – oh bugger! It is then I hear her lumbering towards me. I dive into the car, hit the central locking system then, in my haste, cleverly drop my keys down the side of the gear stick. Cue for loud prolonged scream. Millie has produced a large tree branch at this stage – more like the size of a tree – and proceeds to bash my windscreen with it. And believe me, she isn't as funny as Basil in Fawlty Towers!

After finally retrieving my keys with shaky hands I am off like a bat out of hell, which is quite appropriate for that dark and demonic environment, straight to the nearest pub for a swift double. Who ever said temping was easy!

Like I said, some things you just can't forget. Anyway, I rang the agency, and told them the situation. Jacqui, who was over this particular booking, said, "Oh, Jan, letting us down at the eleventh hour, couldn't you go back?" I had done eleven weeks out of twelve and the daft cow wanted me to get my brains bashed in, all for fulfilling her assignment, not to mention making money for her agency. Not on your Nellie! Head of nursing was on my side when I phoned her the next day to explain. It was nearly my funeral, which leads me on nicely to my next barking assignment, dear reader!

One day, I am going to be truly sick by this snotty-nosed man that I have the misfortune to sit next to on the train. On quite a few occasions I have been on the train first and he seems to seek me out. It's a bit like Jasper Carrot's 'Nutter on the Bus' sketch. When I see him coming down the aisle, I usually glue my face to the window and stare out in the hope that he won't see me or sit next to me – then lo and behold, bonk, he's thrown himself down into the next seat to me sniffing and snotting all over the place.

It's not so much that I'm obsessed with colds and flu in a small environment like a train. Well, it is really, and let's face it we all catch something sometime or another. It's the disgusting fact that when Snot Bag blows his nose, he does it so loudly and then proceeds to leisurely open his handkerchief wide and peer into it to see its colourful contents. That's when I could throw up! Why doesn't he hold it up to the light and really have a good look, or share it with the rest of the passengers by passing it around?

On one particular journey, I felt so close to vomiting, having actually caught sight of its contents, that I made the excuse that I was meeting someone at Horsforth then stood and walked to the end of the train, swaying and recovering. After staggering off at the station I was a bit off guard as I met large numbers of

people shoving and pushing me along. We were like salmon, going one way up a river, not
too dissimilar to shopping in Ikea, where everyone goes at such a ferocious speed having to stick to the strip of hard flooring that meanders its way through the store to keep you on the right track. The force of other humans hurtling behind me can make me feel quite giddy.

Anyway, suffice it to say, incidents like that make me feel like throwing up. But where I was going for my next assignment had lots of beds so I suppose I could recover by having a bit of a lie down.

Assignment 4 : Four Weddings and a Funeral

I was the PA at a local 100-bedroomed hotel. Apart from being the PA, I was also the HR Manager to approximately 75 staff, nearly all of

whom were Russian, Latvian, Lithuanian, Polish and Spanish young kids, and they were a fabulous bunch. On the whole I felt like mother hen, but that is probably what I am best at doing, looking after and being very hands-on.

The whole atmosphere was completely up my street, lots going on, busy and bustling, never a dull moment and never the same day. There were also plenty of perks to the job such as suits, dry cleaning, lunch provided and delicious fresh coffee whenever we wanted.

There were very few members of staff I didn't get on with … on second thoughts, there was just one! I have always made it my intention to get on with all personalities but there will always be one I'll never forget; she was young, arrogant and just plain stroppy. In a nutshell, too young to cope with the dizzy heights of a managerial position, being aged just 21. It went to her head and this was the one I aptly named Cruella De Ville (without the Dalmatian dogs of course).

When she couldn't cope, and often her face would become deep scarlet, she was off-hand with her staff and, even worse with the clientele that used to stay at the hotel. Remember, Cruella, they paid our damn wages!

One weekend we had quite a lot of elderly people on tour staying with us. And although my office was off the main reception area I would always pop out and have a quick word with them, see if they had slept all right, enjoyed their evening meal, that sort of thing. I used to run my own 10-bedroomed B&B in the North Yorkshire Moors, so nattering always came easy to me. And clients DO appreciate this! Anyway, on with my memories of my time there.

It's the second day of the tour and Edna and Ernie, an elderly couple I had particularly befriended, or maybe they'd just latched on to me, collar me at lunch time and ask would I like to join them for a cup of tea outside. That week we'd had had some lovely wooden garden furniture delivered and it looked quite impressive outside the front of the hotel, so I decided to join them there during my lunch break. We had a lovely half hour's natter before finally I say I have to go and do the banking, etc., and get back to work, but most likely I will see them later that evening after one of their little jaunts around the Yorkshire Dales.

The following morning, I am summoned to the General Manager's office and was informed that I had been seen eating outside with guests. I confess I did so albeit during my lunch break and ask if there is a problem. I am told that if I carry on like that the kitchen porters will be out there next wearing their KP blue uniforms and that would not look too good! As I didn't wear the KP blue kitchen suits – I always wore dark suits and always looked professional – I never did wear a name badge like many others such as the receptionists and duty managers.

Incidentally, who do you think dropped me in it? Yes, you've guessed it, Cruella. So there's always someone who'll bitch. Mind you, the loveliest bitch of all was our gay assistant General Manager, whom I referred to as Reggie Baby. Now that was a guy who really was a laugh a minute! Oh, yes, and I always laugh when I think of one particular events involving Reg.

On this particular day there's a wedding going on at one end of the hotel and a funeral service going on at the other. Reggie is always dressed impeccably, the way that only gays can.

Mincing about around the hotel, shouting and pointing at the staff to get on with their various jobs. At one end there is a wonderful vibrant wedding with lots of guests, laughter,

good food and drink, and children running around the place. The atmosphere is delightful.

In a smaller and much quieter room at the other end of the hotel is a funeral party. The deceased had reached a ripe old age but the relatives and friends are quiet and subdued, recounting episodes from his past. Dear Reggie is running around like a blue-arsed fly, trying to accommodate everyone's needs, and directing the staff. When he goes to the end where the wedding is being held, his persona is, as you might expect, one of fun and good humour.

When he visits the funeral party, his whole demeanour takes on a completely different aspect; sad, respectfully silent, and with a highly convincing show of sadness. Sad faced, lowered voice with clasped hands with again more than a tinge of sadness.

The hours pass and suddenly Reggie bursts into my office shouting, "Fucking 'ell, Jan, I've just bombed into the funeral party, full of the joys of spring and asked them if they were having a fab time! I was completely confused, thought I was in the wedding do." My jaw drops then I start laughing so loudly that I have to close my office door and dry away my tears.

That had me laughing and laughing for hours; in fact it kept me going for days. To this day I still chuckle when I recall Reggie's faux pas.

Hotel work is mighty difficult, having to perform shifts and dealing with lots of different personalities. It can be very hard for the serving staff, such as waiters and waitresses, especially when they do a late shift and then have to follow it by an early shift the following day. Only the young can do it without feeling the strain. Well, not as much as their older counterparts. Still, I do think I am more suited to this environment as I like it busy, snappy and interesting. Perhaps I should consider owning another B & B. After all, it really was both relaxing and fulfilling. Perhaps one day I will think about it, but I would be very careful who I had as my partner – the Orange Dwarf who was in partnership at the retreat, was a total disaster! I shall not be writing about that character, he might sue me. In fact, between you and me, he regularly tries to sue certain bods but never wins, the silly sod!

Medusa, one of the three Gorgons, whose head was cut off by Perseus and placed in the aegis of Minerva, had the power of turning those who looked on her into stone and sure enough, she got on our train this morning. Her astonishingly dark locks are thick and snake-like and to add to all this beauty are her most amazing, decorative acrylic nails. Each nail is carefully crafted with diagonal diamante strips that catch the light and really make you notice how creative they are!

She wears lots of rings on her slender tanned hands and if you totted them all up, I'm sure you'd find a few thousand quidsworth there! She tends to read a book, and has this absorbed, very smiley face as she tucks into her reading matter. She's obviously reads something that is relatively funny or a magazine strictly for ladies. As she reads, she tends to play and twiddle with the odd snake and by the time she gets to Leeds, her hair is completely alive and out of control, which looks slightly interesting.

I often wonder where she might work with this freedom of wild hair, long nails and trendy clothing. Envy creeps in as I'm short haired, although I do spike it up from time to time and put the odd subtle pink strand in it, not too dazzling or brash, or I'd upset many or just not get those sort-after temp jobs (not). I admire people who can just be themselves and are expressive, but her looks would not go down too well in a solicitor's' office, perhaps I should just go do it anyway and become a little more trendy! Perhaps my actor friend Henry is right; "Be more expressive, Jan, get out of the box, or out of your tree maybe, but just go out and be different," he says.

Assignment 5 : Our Henry

Henry is a fellow train traveller. He's very talented, an out-of- work Shakespearean actor luvvie that I see from time to time on assignments. Like all young Thespians, Henry is awaiting for his big break, eager to unleash his talents on the public, frustrated that he has to do administration work to pay the bills, food, and rent, not to mention his penchant for weed. Yes, he's let me know on many occasions that he is finally going to kick the habit. Yeah, right ...

Six foot two, tall, dark and very handsome. In fact, you don't often get tall actors, they are usually small in stature, large in ego, too many insecurities and some crap at their craft! My apologies to good small actors such as Dustin Hoffman, for example; I would go to dinner with you anytime. Okay, I know I'm digressing but small men do have problems. I should know, remember the Orange Dwarf? But that, as I said earlier, is another story and quite a long one at that! (ex second husband and final one I hope)

Henry chats incessantly, hands waving during every moment of the dialogue and exchange of ideas in which we engage, mainly on our train journey, letting me know at every twist and turn that life is just not fair and that he should have had his big break by now. And do you know something? I agree with him!

"The thing is, Henry," I constantly remind him, "never give up." I'm sure that it helps but even if it doesn't, I know he'll make it eventually. Besides his interesting facial expressions, his permanently furrowed brow and a larger-than-life personality, he also finds ways to wile away the time during his most boring assignments, so that monotony and boredom do not ravage the very fibre of his grey matter and make him brain-dead forever, like the rest of the inmates. "Never mind, Henry," I try to console him, "you've always got your murder mystery weekends to throw yourself at."

When we meet on the train, which isn't that often, we always gabble away at a hundred miles an hour, telling each other which are our favourite characters in the workplace, the most boring part of the assignment and what naughty things we could dream up and possibly get away with. And I have to say, Henry is a master when it comes to that sort of thing!

One day, when he had nothing else to do, he decided to go and have a kip under the boardroom table. Dishevelled and rat-faced from the previous boozy evening, he lay there pale and comatosed, teetering on the edge of a gigantic vomit. Slowly the mammoth volcanic feeling in his gut subsided enough to enable him to doze off for a while, only to be awoken by a cacophony of shuffling feet, droning voices and the odd fist beating on the table. The dreaded two hour board meeting had begun. Oh, bollocks!

Fear. Terror. Frozen limbs. Thumping heart. Then a smack of such a strong surge of adrenalin that his whole skin positively stung! "How the hell do I get out of this! Think, think. YES, I'll act my way out of it. Slowly shuffling along on his back, he inched his way down the carpet to the foot of the gigantic table, which resembled his soon-to-be coffin. Death was surely imminent …

As he relayed the story, flapping about with excitement, I started to conjure up the scene and screamed with laughter as I imagined this massive lad under the table, inching his way to the end, and thinking it might be a grisly one at that!

"I would have got away with it, Jan," said Henry, "except this gormless prat dropped his glass tumbler on my head, just as I was going to make my escape and with the mother of all hangovers, I let out a yelp. That was that, I was sent packing, packing being the operative word, as I am now working in a warehouse. It's so beneath me, darling. No ... thinking about it, I prefer the salt of the earth warehouse types, not boring pen pushers." Poor Henry!

I hope when Henry makes it and he's on the big screen and all these sad, grey, power-mad, office types come and see him. I am sure that there will be a slight glow of envy at this talented, famous, misunderstood genius of an actor!

Assignment 5 So this is it!

I had a terrible nightmare last night. In the nightmare I am standing feeling miserable on the cold and rainy platform in Harrogate. When the train pulls in I board it in slow motion, observing everything in great detail. It felt quite scary. All of a sudden there is a terrible noise and commotion. Utter chaos in fact. Then there I am, lying prostrate on the carriage floor. Monsieur du Pont is force feeding me camembert cheese as he pins me down in the centre of the aisle. People shouting abuse at him for being such a perv for staring at them!

Medusa is joining in and is trying to save me from his grip, with a big weighty knee on his shoulder. The hair snakes are behaving very badly, flying around at an alarming speed, being more of a hindrance than a help. Mustard Coat, in her desire to assist, is sitting on my chest and squashing every bit of air out of me until I choke and cough and splutter little slithers of cheese all over the windows.

In the end we cannot see the lovely country side and all of this is being photographed by my good friend Ali, photographer for the Harrogate Advertiser, who roars with laughter at the commotion and furore and screeches at me with delight that it was much more fun than our time spent at the Losang Dragpa Buddhist Monastery at Todmorden. What did she mean!

Henry was reciting, "To be, or not to be, that is the question." "Shut up Henry, for God's sake. GET ME OUT OF HERE." I awake with a massive jolt.

I believe all this delirium came about because today is the day I start my permanent new job. My God, I'm panicking! Tossing and turning, last night in bed, toing and froing with sweaty hair plastered to my head. If I woke up once I must have woke up a thousand times in the night, double-checking to see if my alarm clock had gone off! It's odd how the psyche can play up, especially when you haven't had a good night's kip.

So that's about it. I won't be sorry to leave my temping days behind, no more scruffy offices, a voice that is now heard, which is mine. Time off if I want it.

Nor will I be sorry to leave the insecurities behind. Let's face it, it will be a bigger salary, I will be able to have proper relationships, lasting relationships with people at work, and not being the invisible temp. Instead, I shall be accepted. I sound a sad creature, don't I? I don't care. Oh yes, and I'll get to go on all the team building exercises too. And the away days, and guess who'll get to organise them all, Yes, yours truly! So permanency here I come, with a big smile.

© **Jan Coates – The Other Side of the Office**